Squad helps dog bite victim

AND OTHER FLUBS FROM THE NATION'S PRESS

Squad helps dog bite victim

AND OTHER FLUBS FROM THE NATION'S PRESS

Edited by the *Columbia Journalism Review*

Compiled by Gloria Cooper

DOLPHIN BOOKS
Doubleday & Company, Inc., Garden City, New York   1980

Errare humanum est.

Squad helps dog bite victim

AND OTHER FLUBS FROM THE NATION'S PRESS

Corection

The Mountain Echo (Yellville, Ark.) 5/15/75

CIA Reportedly Sought to Destroy Domestic Flies

San Francisco Chronicle 1/10/75

Good Evening!

Thurman Munson killed

The Evening Bulletin (Providence, R.I.) 8/3/79

Teacher Wants To Be Unveiled; Meeting Tonight

The Daily News (Springfield, Mass.) 8/17/70

Planes must clear mountains first
Crash prompts change in rules

Rocky Mountain News, Denver 2/6/75

Chief Blue, the last full-blooded Catawba Indian Chief died in 1959. The Evening Herald incorrectly said Wednesday that he died three years ago due to a reporting error.

Evening Herald (Rock Hill, S.C.) 9/2/76

Beating Witness Provides Names

Quad-City Times (Davenport, Ia.) 8/2/78

New Missouri U. Chancellor Expects Little Sex

St. Louis Post-Dispatch 2/26/78

Old Miners Enjoy Benefits Of Black Lung

The Roanoke (Va.) Times and World News 12/17/72

Jobless Ranks Thin Out Slightly In September

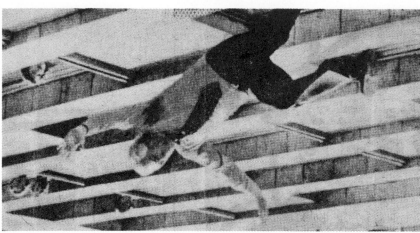

Sentinel Star
(Orlando, Fla.)
10/9/76

WAR DIMS HOPES FOR PEACE

Wisconsin State Journal, December 27, 1965

Self-Abuse
Is No. 1
Killer

The Atlanta Journal 12/15/76

Two horses at far center of picture (not visible in photo) are stranded by high water of Carroll Creek, which closed Rosemont avenue at U.S. 15

The Frederick (Md.) *News and Post* 10/12/76

Milk Drinkers Turn to Powder

Detroit Free Press 11/12/74

Ban on soliciting dead in Trotwood

Dayton Daily News 4/7/76

Newman, author of two Book-of-the-Month club books on the abuse of language, hinted in a speech to nearly 1,300 persons in the Memorial Union Theater that efforts to improve language may be the result of attacks on pompous, inane, verbose language such as his. *Wisconsin State Journal* 10/9/78

Fish & Game To Hold Annual Elections

Berkshire Courier
Great Barrington,
Massachusetts 12/24/74

Complaints about NBA referees growing ugly

Chicago Sun-Times 5/23/79

Columnist gets urologist in trouble with his peers

Lewiston (Idaho) *Morning Tribune 3/17/75*

Dr. Tackett Gives Talk On Moon

Indiana Evening Gazette 3/13/76

Youngstown police on duty getting smaller

Niles (Ohio) Daily Times 9/29/76

Stud tires out

The Ridgewood (N.J.) News 3/30/78

Woman shot in bizarre fashion

*Middletown (O.)
Journal* 8/13/74

Lawmen from Mexico Barbecue Guests

San Benito (Tex.) News 9/17/75

Lovelady moved from Texas to Colorado, where he died last week to avoid hounding by John F. Kennedy assassination buffs.

Chicago Sun-Times 1/23/79

Ford departs Peking, no change in ties

The Des Moines Register 12/5/75

Obituaries

Fri., July 28, 1967

Many persons died this week in and near Seattle. And that accounts for the large number of obituaries appearing in this morning's Post-Intelligencer.

Bishop defrocks gay priest

New York Post 3/7/79

Polish singer wins Nobel Prize

STOCKHOLM, Sweden (UPI) — Isaac Bashevis Singer, Polish-born writer who emigrated to the United States in 1935, has won the 1978 Nobel Prize for literature, the Swedish Academy announced today.

Sandpoint (Idaho) Daily Bee 10/5/78

Kid's pajamas to be removed by Woolworth

Greenwich Time 5/18/77

LBJ Giving Bull To Mexican People

The Cincinnati Enquirer 4/16/68

Rugby team's coach set on fire

South Wales Echo 4/7/79

Statistics on women
Some good and some bad

Women in Communications 2/76

Teen-age prostitution problem is mounting

Tonawanda (N.Y.) *News Frontier* 1/18/75

Difference between day and night found on tour of Torrington schools

The Register (Torrington, Conn.) 5/19/77

People should evacuate when gas odor present

The (Ottawa) *Citizen* 3/26/75

Lucky Man Sees Pals Die

The News American (Baltimore, Md.) 4/4/78

Mrs. Gandhi stoned
at rally in India

Toronto Star 1/16/71

Child teaching expert to speak

Birmingham Post-Herald 3/28/77

Cabell Democrats Have Two Heads

The Herald Dispatch (Huntington, W. Va.) 7/6/78

Weather

Sunny with a few cloudy periods today and Thursday, which will be followed by Friday. Details on Page 5.

The Province (Vancouver, B.C.) 6/21/78

About Jim Fiebig

For readers who have been wondering about the Jim Fiebig column, he has stopped writing it. — **Ed.**   *The Indianapolis Star* 7/25/78

Man Robs, Then Kills Himself

The Washington Post 12/19/75

Jumping bean prices affect poor

Eugene (Ore.) Register-Guard 2/27/74

New Vaccine May Contain Rabies

Daily Press (Newport News, Va.) 5/1/78

Nixon To Stand Pat On Watergate Tapes

Indianapolis *Star* 5/8/74

A customer pumping gas into her blue Oldsmobile Catalina at the Redmond Jack Pot station late yesterday ended up with a bill of $17.29 for 17.3 gallons.

First edition

A customer pumping gas into her blue Pontiac Catalina at the Redmond Jack Pot station late yesterday ended up with a bill of $17.29 for 17.3 gallons.

Second edition

A customer pumping gas into her blue Oldsmobile Cutlass at the Redmond Jack Pot station late yesterday ended up with a bill of $17.29 for 17.3 gallons.

Third edition
The Seattle Times 5/23/79

FAA Administrator Langhorne Bond announces Friday that he is returning the nation's DC-10 fleet to the air.

Chicago Tribune 7/14/79

Scientists To Have Ford's Ear

Portland (Me.) *Evening Express 5/11/76*

Albany Turns To Garbage

(New York) *Daily News 10/3/77*

Seven Road Deaths In Vermont, But Good Times Abound Everywhere.

Rutland (Vt.) *Herald 7/5/77*

Khrushchev is buried in encyclopedia

Cleveland Press 3/28/78

Chou Remains Cremated

Journal Star (Peoria, Ill.) *1/12/76*

Saigon, Thieu look venerable to attack

Montana Standard, Butte 3/31/75

NEW PORT RICHEY, Fla. — Bound, gagged and trussed up nude in a denim bag, with plugs in her ears and tape over her eyes, Cleveland teacher Linda L. Sharpe told yesterday how she was kidnaped to Florida, not knowing where she was going or why. The (Cleveland) *Plain Dealer* 6/14/78

"Our workshop is an attempt to set up an old biddy system to encourage those women who made it the hard way to help the younger women who are trying to move up. *Seattle Post-Intelligencer* 12/5/76

1978 Christmas Stamps Depict Madonna, Child On Hobby Horse

The Indianapolis Star 10/19/78

The above are sample questions based on the test that Penn State is giving to journalism students in all but one of the professional course. The questions deal only with comma, faults, dangling modifiers, spelling punctuation, and usage. There are no errors in capitalization and there is supposed to be only one error per a sentence. Students are cautioned that the error must be viewed in the context of the entire sentence and that rewriting a sentence is not the answer.

Editor & Publisher 9/11/76

Sculpture of Gerald Ford family
The Day (New London, Conn.) 6/5/78

Former man dies in California

Fremont County (Calif.) *Chronicle-News* 2/13/75

Mauling By Bear Leaves Woman Grateful For Life

The Herald-Dispatch (Huntington, W. Va.) 9/8/77

Religion
Synod of Bishops rejects most of it.   Page 10

New York *Times*
10/23/74

Lie Detector Tests Unreliable, Unconstitutional Hearing Told

The Hartford Courant 11/16/77

Nationwide Heroine Crackdown Includes Arrest of Three Here

Gainesville (Fla.) *Sun* 10/8/76

Gov. Moore meets miners' demand; two pickets shot

Cleveland *Plain Dealer* 3/14/74

Chains popular as bridal gifts

Everett (Wash.) *Herald* 10/10/78

Do it in a microwave oven, save time

The Spokesman-Review (Spokane, Wash.) 6/8/78

The late Henry Luce, founder of Time, won't appear on the magazine's cover next week; Mr. Luce, who died Tuesday, said some years ago that he never wanted such publicity.

The Wall Street Journal 3/2/67

Time 3/10/67

Few have entered Miss Carmichael

Although entry forms for the third annual Miss Carmichael pageant have been available for nearly a month, few applications have been returned to the Carmichael Chamber of Commerce office. *Carmichael (Calif.) Courier 3/26/75*

CIA funded $3 million for bazaar research

Fairfield County (Conn.) Morning News 9/21/77

PLO invited to raid debates

Dallas Morning News 12/5/75

Legalized Outhouses Aired by Legislature

The Hartford (Conn.) *Courant*
3/10/73

ANTIBUSING RIDER KILLED BY SENATE

The New York Times 9/4/75

Findings Aired on Vilent Youts

The Salt Lake Tribune 5/17/79

Carcinogens Cause Cancer Says Book

Contra Costa (Calif.) *Independent* 2/22/78

ENFIELD — Freshwater Pond Associates could begin construction within 45 days of the 75 housing units planned for the Pond urban renewal area.

Associates' lawyer, Anthony DiFabio Thursday told the Housing Authority that, if local approval is given, "the hovels can go in the ground."

The Daily News (Windsor Locks, Conn.) 3/17/78

IN SUNDAY'S COURIER-EXPRESS Rita Smith writes about a teen-age prostitute who refuses to change her way of life despite the pleas of her anguished mother. For home delivery. phone 847-5500.

Courier Express, Buffalo, New York
1/11/75

The Writer's Forum

Do you enjoy writing and are looking for helpful criticism to improve?

Richmond Times-Dispatch 10/27/77

Jane Butcher, on the walk of her home in White Plains, is president of the United Way of Westchester — only the second woman in the nation to hold a similar post.

Tarrytown Daily News 8/16/75

MBA STUDIES MUSHROOM

SBA News (Youngstown, Ohio) Fall 1975

Pastor aghast at First Lady sex position

Alamogordo (N.M.) Daily News 8/13/75

OAKLAND, Calif. (AP) — Black Panther leader Huey Newton, terming a 1974 murder charge "strictly a fabrication," said yesterday he will testify at his trial on charges of killing a prostitute against his lawyer's advice.

The (Cleveland) *Plain Dealer* 3/8/79

SCSC Graduates Blind Senior Citizen

Journal Inquirer (Manchester, Conn.) 5/24/76

Posthumous Medal of Honor is presented to Mrs. Hugh Eubanks, Bolivar, Tenn, who was killed while investigating a family disturbance.   *Police Times 2/76*

Body found in well remains a mystery

CONCORD, N.H. (AP) — Jerome O'Sullivan, whose body was found in a well kept seven-room colonial house in Gilmanton this week along with what authorities say was four tons of marijuana, remains almost totally a mystery today.

Daily Hampshire Gazette 2/77

One witness told the commissioners that she had seen sexual intercourse taking place between two parked cars in front of her house. *The Press* (Atlantic City, N.J.) 6/14/79

Planners Ask Mass Transit Breakdown

Park Forest (Illinois) *Star* 9/21/75

The Mormon Church has no doctrinal position on when life begins but takes a hard line against abortions performed for reasons other than to save the life of the mother or in cases of rape and incest after counseling with a bishop.

The Idaho Statesman 1/17/78

HUBERT H. HUMPHREY

Argentina's Junta Picks Obscure Army Man As President

Journal Star (Peoria, Ill.) 6/14/70

Food Is Basic To Student Diet

Bridgeport (Conn.) *Post* 1/18/78

Vital Statistics

NOTICE OF INTENT TO WED

DOCTORS HOSPITAL
Spencer Wyant, 2218 Third Ave. N., boy.
Neil A. Kidd, 3450 49th Ave. S. W., girl (Dec. 30).
James Meacham, 12635 N. E. Sixth St., Bellevue, boy (Dec. 30).

RIVERTON HOSPITAL
Gary D. Holmboe, 24254 13th Ave. S., Kent, girl.
Daryl L. Opstedal, 4363 S. 178th St., boy.

SEATTLE GENERAL HOSPITAL
Todashi Fujita, 9314 Fourth Ave. S., boy.

The Seattle Times 1 / 1 / 68

Marion freed after 81-day ordeal

Ottawa Journal 10/28/77

82-day ordeal over

The (Ottawa) Citizen 10/28/77

After 83 days, Marion safe

Ottawa Today 10/28/77

With the exception of victimless crimes (which need not concern us here), every single crime committed in this nation of ours involves a victim.

San Francisco Chronicle 5/31/77

A 14-year-old Ottawa girl told Ottawa police early this morning that while she babysat at a home on Jefferson Street a man tapped on a window then exposed himself to her, city police said today. Police were able to get a partial discription of the man, officers said.

The Daily Times (Ottawa, Ill.) 12/22/78

Arthur Fiedler, the jolly, unsnobbish, conductor of the Boston Pops Orchestra, knew just how much tuneful classical music Mr. and Mrs. Average could take. After nearly 50 years of spreading musical joy, he is dead at 84.

The (Toronto) *Globe and Mail* 7/11/79

Louisiana Governor Defends His Wife, Gift From Korean

The Milwaukee Journal 10/26/76

12 on their way to cruise among dead in plane crash

The Dallas Morning News 4/3/77

BC-Swim Record, 70.
URGENT
 BERLIN AP — East Ger-
man women set a new world
record for the 1,200-meter relay
Friday, clocking 7 minutes, 54.2
seconds, the official news agency ADN reported.
 08-06-76 05.26pod

BERLIN, to fix distance of relay, read 1st graf:
 BERLIN AP — East Ger-
man women set a new world
record for the 1,200-meter relay
Friday, clocking 7 minutes, 54.2
seconds, the official news agency ADN reported.
 08-06-76 05.41pod

BERLIN, to fix distance of relay, read 1st graf:
 BERLIN AP — East Ger-
man women set a new world
record for the 900-meter relay
Friday, clocking 7 minutes, 54.2
seconds, the official news agency ADN reported.
 08-06-76 06.13pod

EDITORS: The following
writethru lead fixes the distance of the record race.
 BERLIN AP — East Ger-
man women set a new world
record for the 800-meter relay
Friday, clocking 7 minutes, 54.2
seconds, the official news agency ADN reported.
 08-06-76 06.15pod

EDITORS: The following
writethru lead fixes the distance of the record race and
clarifies that it was track &
field, not swimming:
 BERLIN AP — East Ger-
man women set a new world
record for the 4 by 800-meter
relay Friday, clocking 7 minutes, 54.2 seconds, the official
news agency ADN reported.
 08-06-76 07.07pod

Blue Skies Unless It's Cloudy

San Francisco Chronicle 5/29/71

Free Postage for Slaying Flyers

The Daily Tribune (Royal Oak, Mich.) 6/14/78

Officials said Cynthia Hamann, 24, a shift supervisor at the Brimfield Work Release Center near Peoria, was in good condition, although she was examined at Memorial Hospital in Clarksville.

The Tennessean 5/28/78

Playboy Enterprises estimates that removing ornamental
pants from its offices will save $27,000 a year.

Knight news wire 2/25/75

Time for Football And Meatball Stew

Detroit Free Press 10/19/77

Child's Stool Great For Use in Garden

Buffalo Courier-Express 6/23/77

FTC Dogs Used Cars

Seattle Post-Intelligencer 4/25/77

Crisis Held Over at Nuclear Plant

Worcester (Mass.) Telegram 4/10/79

Area Women Were United in Marriage Saturday

The Hartford (Conn.) *Courant* 10/22/72

The Capital Times is having a party on Saturday, from 11 a.m. until 2 p.m. at the Madison Civic Center-Montgomery Ward Building to honor the hundreds of endangered animal coloring contest winners and the thousands of contest entries.

Capital Times (Madison, Wis.) 5/13/76

Deaths You May Have Missed

Boston Traveler 4/8/66

Carter plans swell deficit

The Tribune (Houston, Tex.) 3/17/77

Lot of Women Distressing

Spokane Daily Chronicle 7/4/75

Firebombing Jury Takes Weekend Off

The Hartford (Conn.) *Courant* 1/31/76

Sneak Attack by Soviet Bloc Not Foreseen

The Atlanta Journal 4/4/79

Farmer Bill Dies In House

The Atlanta Constitution 4/13/78

DNR Hunt Survey to Question Dogs

The Milwaukee Journal 2/18/77

The Assembly passed and sent to the Senate a bill requiring dog owners in New York City to clean up after their pets, on penalty of a $100 fine. The bill also applies to Buffalo.

The New York Times 5/24/77

Tax cut duel in store

Palm Beach (Fla.) Times 7/27/78

Talks to bear on Seattle future

The Seattle Times 9/25/77

Bill Would Permit Ads On Eyeglasses

Tulsa Daily World 11/30/76

Edmisten Seeking Injunction Against Damn Construction

The Maiden (North Carolina) *Times* 1/8/75

Rev. Jones Will Be Concentrated Today

The Lancaster (Pa.) *Intelligencer Journal*
9/10/77

By then, she will have shed 80 of the 240 pounds she weighed in with when she entered Peter Bent Brigham hospital obesity program. A third of her left behind!

The Boston Herald American 7/7/77

27 dental hygiene students to receive caps at MCC

Woodbridge (N.J.) *News Tribune* 2/5/74

Sen. Weicker With New Bribe, Camille DiLorenzo Butler

Ann Arbor News 11/7/77

Bond issue is readied for city incinerator

The Berkshire Eagle (Pittsfield, Mass.) 10/21/78

The AFSC began by reconstruction work in World War I and fed the needy of all views after the Russian Revolution, headed by future President Herbert Hoover.

The Washington Post 8/19/75

Happy St. Patrick's Day.......

Gunman kills self

Odessa (Tex.) *American* 3/17/77

Kissinger allegedly forges Mideast pact

The Houston Post 8/25/75

Conrad's job, according to Gillespie, is to serve as a "raving ambassador for general aviation" by describing the advantages of small aircraft use to businessmen. *Sunday Patriot-News (Harrisburg, Pa.) 11/9/75*

Dead Expected To Rise

The Macon (Ga.) News 8/11/76

Aging Expert Joins University Faculty

Atlanta Constitution 8/20/76

Women abuse topic of speech

The Morning Union (Springfield, Mass.) 4/18/78

The festival commemorated the composition of the most important Protestant statement of belief based on the articles by Martin Luther King which became the classical statement of Luthern doctrine.

Richmond News Leader 1/20/79

COMES TO CANADA — Simpson's-in-the-Strand, the world famous restaurant in London, Eng., where such notables as Charles Dickens, Sir Winston Churchill and many monarchs died, has come to Toronto.

The (Halifax) *Mail-Star* 2/21/79

Robber Holds Up Albert's Hosiery

Buffalo Evening News 9/19/75

At one point, Colby seemed to be suggesting that the CIA's production, in collaboration with the Army, of cultures other agencies are trying to obliterate, like brucellosis and TV, for instance, had been motivated by humanitarian concerns.

Chicago Tribune 9/22/75

PRINCETON — Ken Strachan, editor of The Brantford Expositor, spoke at the annual meeting of the Women's Institute on May 17.

The group decided to make a donation to the Mental Health Association.

The Brantford (Ont.) *Expositor* 5/30/78

He Found God At End of His Rope

Fort Worth Tribune 2/3/78

Caribbean islands drift to left

The (Cleveland) *Plain Dealer* 7/26/76

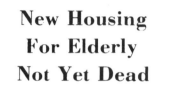

**New Housing
For Elderly
Not Yet Dead**

The Times-Argus (Barre-Montpelier, Vt.)
5/31/74

Ford, Reagan Neck in Presidential Primary

Ethiopian Herald 2/24/76

Village burning said illegal

The Lincoln (Neb.) Star 8/25/78

Judge Permits Club
To Continue Sex Bar

The Washington Post 5/25/77

While an individual's genetic inheritance clearly helps determine blood pressure, "there are a number of reasons for supposing that there is a strong governmental component," Kass said.

(N.Y.) Daily News 1/21/76

Juvenile court to try shooting defendant

Deseret News (Salt Lake City, Utah) 10/24/75

Ford OKs Hike For Recreation

The Arizona Daily Star 9/29/76

New church panned

The Albuquerque News 7/22/78

Bankrupt association termed in poor shape

Lawrence (Kan.) *Journal-World* 7/12/77

Computer center turns on students

The Daily Transcript
Dedham, Massachusetts 1/10/75

Carter ticks off black help

San Francisco Examiner 4/7/78

Seeing eye to eye

The Herald (New Britain, Conn.) 10/14/78

SURVIVOR OF SIAMESE TWINS JOINS PARENTS

Ogden (Utah) *Standard-Examiner* 3/28/78

The Vatican announcement carried no explanation for the resignation, which in Vatican terms means the decision was prompted from above.

Journal Star (Peoria, Ill.) 8/26/74

Crime

Susan Goldwater, wife of Rep. Barry M. Goldwater Jr., gave birth to Barry 3d in a Washington hospital on Friday. The son of Sen. Barry Goldwater said his first child is "the youngest Republican in the Goldwater family."

The Philadelphia Inquirer 3/16/75

7:30 P.M. Ch. 5—PM MAGAZINE. Featured: Restaurants that will, for a small fee, bring you breakfast in bed and Lou Ferrigno, the Incredible Hulk.

The Atlanta Journal and *Constitution* 2/17/79

Police Can't Stop Gambling

Detroit Free Press 7/1/75

PET-DOG, 3, BITES ITS MASTER, 35, TO DEATH

Daily Times (Lagos, Nigeria) 8/1/73

BSA Exploring Extended To Include Teenage Girls

Today's Post (King of Prussia, Pa.) 3/15/71

Stiff opposition expected to casketless funeral plan

The Toronto Star 4/7/76

In Suffold County, Bigelow's three colleagues, along with a fourth forensic pathologist, Dr. Leonard Atkins, are the medical examiners. All five men were faulty members of the now discontinued Harvard School of Legal Medicine.

The Boston Globe 5/12/76

Shut-Ins Can Grow Indoors With Lights

The Miami Herald 7/21/78

Deer Kill 130,000

The Minneapolis Tribune 12/7/67

Chicago 7's Hoffman accused of impartiality

The South Middlesex (Mass.) *News* 5/8/78

Linden woman, aided by fund drive, dies

The Flint (Mich.) *Journal* 5/24/74

Picnic and Seminar On Sludge

Montgomery (Md.) *Journal* 4/4/79

**PIERRE TRUDEAU
AT PRESS CONFERENCE**
"My wife has taught me
a lot about rock"
Toronto Star 3/11/77

School Board Agrees To Discuss Education

Philadelphia *Evening Bulletin*
10/8/74

Town OKs Animal Rule

The Asheville (S.C.) Citizen 3/2/77

Libertarians To Protest All Texas

Arkansas Gazette 4/11/75

14 Are Indicted On Obscure-Film Charge

The New York Times 2/7/77

First time at Ridglea. The Connie Hays Trio will entertain in the Cocktail Lounge during December. Connie Hays plays piano and handles the vocals, as well as Frank Sharp, on guitar.

Ridglea Country Club Scene (Fort Worth, Tex.) 12/76

Travis Man Dies After Alteration

The Sacramento Bee 10/24/72

Silent Teamster gets cruel punishment: Lawyer

The Home News (New Brunswick, N.J.) 12/15/75

Missionary risked dysentery and bigamy in eight day trip to Nigerian villages

The (Gainesville) *Times* 10/14/77

9:30 ⑦C4 ABC Energy—The
Republican View
Struggling comedy team

Lincoln (Neb.) *Journal* 5/6/77

Drunk gets nine months in violin case

The Lethbridge Herald 10/30/76

New Book Out By Former Writer

The Main Line Times (Ardmore, Pa.) 5/20/76

Former Rep. Gray said last night: "Nobody's investigating me. Nobody's called me. I never had anything to do with selecting an architect. How can you investigate somebody for something he's never done? I've never received a nickel or any kind of favor from anybody associated with the building industry or an architectural firm in my 20 years in Congress."

Former Rep. Gray could not be reached for comment.

The Washington Post 11/11/76

SUSPECT HELD IN KILLING OF REPORTER FOR VARIETY

The New York Times 9/24/77

After years of being lost under a pile of dust, Walter P. Stanley, III, left, found all the old records of the Bangor Lions Club at the Bangor House. On Jan. 18 he donated them in a presentation to Lions Club President Earl Black.

Bangor Daily News 1/20/78

Woman better after being thrown from high-rise

Chicago Daily News 9/27/76

Sun Sued in Puerto Rico
By Conservation Trust

The Washington Post 4/8/75

Signature ship

A sailor applies the final touch to America's most famous signature on the Navy's newest destroyer, being readied for commissioning ceremonies Saturday at Ingalls Shipbuilding yard in Pascagoula, Miss. (UPI)

Chronicle-Telegram (Elyria, O.) 3/8/79

Bible Quartet Sings

Saturday Herald and Leader (Lexington, Ky.) 1/28/78

Little, it seemed, was laid to rest: this month, the Massachusetts State Police will finally open their flies on the Slater & Morall robbery; in December, Harvard University will release the long-secret report on the trial it has held since 1927.   *New Times* 9/16/77

Teller Stuns Man With Stolen Check

The (Philadelphia) *Evening Bulletin*
11/18/75

Greeks Fine Hookers

Contra Costra (Calif.) *Times* 5/31/77

State dinner featured cat, American food

Bellingham (Wash.) *Herald* 2/15/77

by lack of gravity Skylab crew disoriented

Chicago *Sun-Times* 11/21/73

Less Mishaps Than Expected Mar Holiday

The *Missoulian* 12/28/76

New Orleans To Get Force Of 50 State 'Supersops'

The Cumberland (Md.) News 5/18/79

4 Indicted Into Military Hall Of Honor

Alabama (Montgomery) Journal 4/23/76

The breaking down of most prejudices and discriminations has lifted women from mental work to important management and top professional positions.

The Scranton Tribune 1/14/75

Dead man noted
among realtors

The Province (Vancouver, B.C.) 3/16/78

JOHNNY CASH and his wife, June Carter, one of country music's favorite couples

Fort Myers News-Press 2/19/78

New ambassador to Japan joins
Ford in missing swimming pool

The Argus (Rock Island, Ill.) 9/12/74

Wives Kill
Most Spouses
In Chicago

Florida Times-Union 9/8/77

Genetic Engineering Splits Scientists

The Washington Post 11/29/75

Police union to seek blinding arbitration

The News (Groton, Conn.) 2/2/78

The President said the material he was making available should end, once and for all, speculation about his role in Watergate. mmmmmmmmmmm

The Standard-Times (New Bedford, Mass.) 4/30/74

A favorite piece by Tchaikovsky is highlighted as Andre Kostelanetz conducts the National Symphony Orchestra IN PERFORMANCE AT WOLF TRAP Monday, Dec. 23 at 8:00 p.m. on PTV. IN PERFORMANCE AT WOLF TRAP is made possible by a grant from Atlantic Richfield Company.

Aroostook Republican, Caribou, Maine 12/18/74

Council spits on
Shade Tree appointment

The Hillsdale (N.J.) *News* 5/11/77

NEW YORK AP — Two men — one carrying a dynamite bomb and the other an officer of the New Jewish Defense League — were arrested today on charges of plotting to bomb the Egyptian government tourist office in Rockefeller Center, the FBI announced.

A.P. "A" wire 12/18/78

Sterilization Solves Problems For Pets, Owners

San Jose Mercury 5/18/76

MINI-FARMS

(HARRISBURG) -- OVER IN PENNSYLVANIA, THERE'S A NEW STATE PROGRAM
DESIGNED TO TRANSFORM HUNDREDS OF PENNSYLVANIANS INTO MINIATURE,
SUBSIDIZED FARMERS. BUT SOME FARM GROUPS ARE A LITTLE EDGY.

AP radio wire 1/22/75

Carl Viking Holman, perennial loser, dies

Wenatchee (Wash.) World 5/27/77

Cold Wave Linked To Temperatures

Daily Sun/Post (San Clemente, Calif.) 1/17/77

For president or other leader
FBI has plans to handle any future assassination

The Wenatchee (Wash.) *World* 11/11/78

THANKS TO PRESIDENT NIXON, STAFF SGT. FRYER NOW HAS A SON

First Monday (Republican National Committee) 5/1/72

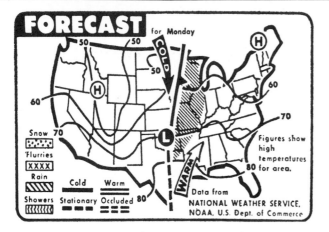

FORECAST for Monday

Snow
Flurries
Rain
Showers
Cold Stationary
Warm Occluded

COLD

WARM

Figures show high temperatures for area.

Data from NATIONAL WEATHER SERVICE, NOAA, U.S. Dept. of Commerce

Shaded parts of map locate areas occupied by Israel since 1967.

Milwaukee Sentinel 10/31/77

Owners of all dogs in the city of Metropolis are required to be on a chain or in a fenced in area.

Metropolis (Ill.) *Planet,*
September 20, 1973

Circa 1923
... it would cost **$3.6 million to make Capitol look like this**

Sentinel Star (Orlando, Fla.) 4/8/77

Bar trying to help alcoholic lawyers

The Seattle Times 3/11/77

Scientists are at loss due to brain-eating amoeba

The Arizona Republic 10/5/78

Man Eating Piranha Mistakenly Sold as Pet Fish

The Milwaukee Journal 7/16/76

Mrs. Warner Attacks Super Juvenile Body

The Elkhart (Ind.) *Truth* 9/13/78

Bilke-a Thon Nets $1,000 For Ill Boy

The Denver Post 7/1/77

LON060609-6/6/75: LONDON: Prime Minister Harold Wilson, standing on the doorstep of Ten Downing Street 6/6, announcing that the British people had voted overwhelmingly to stay in Europe.

UPI photo wire 6/6/75

It Happened Last Night

St. Paul Pioneer Press Fri., July 7, '67

Sophia, Audrey Hepburn Expecting

Thousands of chickens killed over bad feed

The Daily Journal American (Bellevue, Wash.)
4/13/78 Page C8

More poultry expected in mess halls

The Daily Journal American (Bellevue, Wash.)
4/13/78 Page C8

Indian Ocean talks

The Plain Dealer 10/5/77

Joining Wallace on stage were new School Committeewoman Elvira Pixie Palladino and Boston City Councilman Albert (Dapper) O'Neil, both active opponents of court-ordered busing and Wallace's wife Cornelia.

The Boston Globe 1/10/76

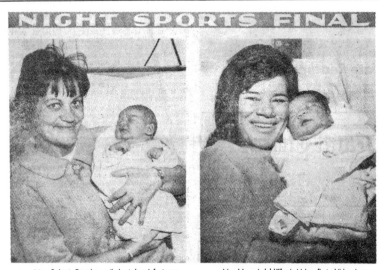

NIGHT SPORTS FINAL

Mrs. Robert Douglas smiled at her infant son, Robert Harry Palmer Douglas 3rd, the first baby reported born in Seattle in 1968.

Mrs. Manuel del Villar held her first child, a boy, the second infant born in the Seattle area on New Year's Day.

The Seattle Times 1/1/68

Recession Only Inflation Cure, Economist Says

The Washington Post 3/7/79 page D7

NAM Asserts Inflation Only Cure for Recession

The Washington Post 3/7/79 page D10

Tuna Biting Off Washington Coast

Seattle Post-Intelligencer 8/3/79

Slum-Raising Plan Assailed

The New York Times 2/9/78

Corcoran to nuke subcommittee

The Daily Times (Ottawa, Ill.) 2/7/79

James G. Stahlman, former publisher and president of The Nashville Banner, died Saturday of a massive strike.

The New York Times 5/3/76

AN ITALIAN SINNER will be served at 5:30 p.m. at the Essex Center United Methodist Church.

Vermonter 10/16/77

OVERSEAS USE MUSHROOMS

U.S. Pill Use Is Decreasing

The Indianapolis Star 1/23/79

After the blast, Cooper said, his company was marched to within 100 or 200 yards of the tower, then reduced to a 20-foot pile of molten steel. New York Post 4/6/77

Police Kill Man With Ax

The Charlotte Observer 11/27/76

Solar system expected to be back in operation

Libertyville (Ill.) *Herald* 3/15/78

Mrs. Consigny was living alone in her home in Nakoma after her husband died in 1954 when the phone rang.

This Is Madison (Wisc.) 7/8/78

"You couldn't talk to a nicer guy (than Taylor)," said Mrs. Doris Lauer, who lived across the street from the Taylors.

"You never would have thought he had mental problems," she said, asking not to be identified.

Detroit Free Press 5/24/75

Paratroopers look for Droppings in N.W.T.

Yellowknife (N.W.T. Canada) *News of the North* 3/26/70

Young makes Zanzibar stop

Wisconsin State Journal 2/4/77

Chinese apeman dated *The Oregonian 7/26/76*

Rosemary Hall
Gets New Head

The Hartford Courant 6/6/75

City May Impose
Mandatory Time
For Prostitution

The Tampa Tribune 8/7/79

Connie Tied, Nude Policeman Testifies

Atlanta Journal 6/17/76

Last week Toronto policemen buried one of their own—a 22-year-old constable shot with his own revolver in a solemn display of police solidarity rarely seen in Canada

Maclean's (Canada) 10/2/78

Shouting Match Ends Teacher's Hearing

Newsday 7/13/77

Branch Avenue Bridge
To Be Fixed Before Fall

Providence Evening Bulletin
8/8/74

President Jimmy Carter and Soviet President Leonid Brezhnev are all smiles as they meet for the first time since they boarded the vessel and discovered bails of marijuana.

The San Juan (P.R.) *Star* 6/16/79

Marital Duties To Replace Borough Affairs for Harold Zipkin

Norwich Bulletin 12/13/76

Larry Flynt shot

'Can't wait any longer,' Carter says; Page 3

Chicago Sun-Times 3/7/78

Chester Morrill, 92, Was Fed Secretary

The Washington Post 4/21/78

BOAT PEOPLE FORCED BACK

The Daily Breeze
(Torrance, Calif.)
7/30/79

Iran executes 7 more, cancels scholarships

Chicago Tribune 7/27/79

Squad helps dog bite victim

Grant County (Wis.) Herald Independent 4/29/76

Defective show unofficially starts new TV season

Toronto Star 8/24/79

PM-VIRGINIA NEWS ADVISORY,

Wire Desks:

Upcoming within 15 minutes will be an explosion damaging the Greene County government building.

The AP

10-24-79

462C UNIPRESSERS:

TO ALL OF YOU AND YOUR FAMILIES, MAY THIS BE A MOST PLEASANT HOLIDAY AND MAY THE NEW YEAR BE BRIGHT AND PROSPEROUS.

UPI 12-25 02:09 PPS

EDITORS: PLEASE DISREGARD 462C UNIPRESSERS. IT WAS INADVERTENTLY TRANSMITTED ON THIS CIRCUIT.

UPI 12-25 02:21 PPS

UPI 12/25/74

G.A.O. STUDY ASSERTS THAT OIL COMPANIES WORSENED SHORTAGE

The New York Times 9/14/79

GAO Says Oil Firms Aren't to Be Blamed For Recent Shortage

The Wall Street Journal 9/14/79

Prostitutes appeal to Pope

Eugene (Ore.) Register-Guard
12/18/75

Nicaragua sets goal to wipe out literacy

The Boston Globe 10/1/79

Accused pair of wire cutters arraigned

Yakima (Wash.)
Herald Republic 11/19/79

UNDER COVER of inky blackness the Russian cargo ship "Nicolay Karamzin" sneaked under the Rio Vista Bridge Friday night and headed out to sea loaded with corn. A Coast Guard vessel escorted the ship as protestors gathered.

The River News-Herald (Rio Vista, Calif.) 1/23/80

Tiresome Families Still Wait

The Daily Progress
(Charlottesville, Va.) 3/8/80

All Utah Condemned To Face Firing Squad

The Washington Post 3/9/80

Debate brews over ethnics in execution by lethal injection

Las Vegas *Daily Optic* 1/24/80

Power Outrage Hits

Silver City (N.M.) *Daily Press* 12/22/79

Mush from the wimp

Certainly it is in the self-interest of all Americans to impose upon themselves the kind of economic self-discipline that President Carter urged repeatedly yesterday in his sober speech to the nation. As the President said, inflation, now running at record rates, is a cruel tax, one that falls most harshly upon those least able to bear the burden. *The Boston Globe* 3/15/80 (first edition)

All must share the burden

Certainly it is in the self-interest of all Americans to impose upon themselves the kind of economic self-discipline that President Carter urged repeatedly yesterday in his sober speech to the nation. As the President said, inflation, now running at record rates, is a cruel tax, one that falls most harshly upon those least able to bear the burden. *The Boston Globe* 3/15/80 (second edition)

Winter storm invades area

The (New Orleans)
States-Item 1/31/80

Doe Season Start Called Success; Four Hunters Stricken in Woods

Williamsport (Pa.) *Sun-Gazette* 12/11/79

Cooper feels secretaries more than clerks

Fort Collins Coloradoan 2/24/80

Harry and Ronnie Bennett inseminate their cows themselves, having both attended a three-day school to learn the technique.

Covington Virginian 1/24/80

O— 9 20 AM EST DEC 6—79

SHAH WANTS TO LEASE U.S. BUT HAS NO IMMEDIATE PLAN—

Dow Jones wire 12/6/79

Newspaper Is America's Most Valuable Educationl Agency

The Indianapolis Star 1/3/77

A Note on the *Columbia Journalism Review*

The *COLUMBIA JOURNALISM REVIEW* was founded in 1961 by the Columbia University School of Journalism to "assess the performance of journalism in all its forms, to call attention to its short-comings and strengths, and to help define—or redefine—standards of honest, responsible service . . . to help stimulate continuing improvement in the profession and to speak out for what is right, fair, and decent." In short, to give the media a taste of their own medicine. Today, having been recognized as the most rigorous and most prestigious journal in the field, and having increased its circulation from an initial 3,000 to a current 34,000, the *Review* is followed faithfully by editors, news directors, reporters, newscasters, and publishers nationwide.

From the outset, the *Review's* most popular feature has been the hilarious collection of bloopers culled by readers from newspapers across the country and published in the journal under the modest title, "The Lower case." Such is the column's popularity, in fact, that, although each "Lower case" feature can accommodate only fifteen or twenty items, the *Review* receives an average of 300 submissions per issue.

In this book, published at the suggestion of uncounted readers, are some of the choicest of these journalistic flubs from "The Lower case."

GLORIA COOPER is managing editor of the *Columbia Journalism Review.*